Just Play

EASY BEGINNER GUITAR LESSONS FOR KIDS

By Jonny Blackwood & Halah M.

Just Play: Easy Beginner Guitar Lessons for Kids
Learn Guitar Today (w/ online video access)

1st Edition

By Jonny Blackwood & Halah M.

Title page and doodle illustrations by Halah M.

Published by Blackwood Guitarworks

www.blackwoodguitarworks.com

Email: info@blackwoodguitarworks.com

www.justplay-music.com

Published June 2022

ISBN 978-1-989514-03-0

Disclaimer

Table of Contents

Introduction 5

Section 1: About the Guitar 6

    Parts of the Guitar 8

Section 2: Playing Technique 13

    Hand Positions 14

        Picking Technique 17

        Strumming 18

    Tuning 19

        How to Tune the Guitar 21

Section 3: Let's Play! 24

    Picking Exercise 1 26

    Picking Exercise 2 28

Section 4: Chords 30

    The G Chord 31

    The C Chord 33

Section 5: Songs 36

    Are You Sleeping? (Brother John) 37

    Row, Row, Row, Your Boat 39

    Mary Had a Little Lamb 40

    London Bridge is Falling Down 42

    The G7 Chord 43

    Rain, Rain, Go Away 44

    A Tisket, A Tasket 46

    Hush Little Baby 48

    This Old Man 50

    The D7 Chord 52

    The Wheels on the Bus 53

    Itsy Bitsy Spider 55

    He's Got the Whole World in His Hands 56

Hokey Pokey 58

She'll Be Coming 'Round the Mountain 60

When the Saints Go Marching In 62

Happy Birthday to You 64

If You're Happy and You Know It 66

Old MacDonald Had a Farm 68

Twinkle, Twinkle, Little Star 72

You Are my Sunshine 74

The D Chord 76

Down by the Bay 77

Oh! Suzanna 80

Section 6: Additional Lessons 82

Picking Song: Hot Crossed Buns 82

Picking Song: Twinkle, Twinkle Little Star 83

Additional Exercises 85

Picking Exercise 3 85

Picking Exercise 4: The C Scale 85

Picking Exercise 5: The G scale 85

Strumming Exercise 3: Mixed Patterns 86

Strumming Exercise 4: Half-Beats & Mixed Patterns 87

Common Chords Diagrams 88

Practice Chart 91

Certificate of Completion 93

Introduction

Thank you for choosing *Just Play: Easy Beginner Guitar Lessons for Kids!*

The methods in this book are simple, yet practical for young beginners to learn guitar.

In this "easy-guitar" book, you'll learn all the basics, such as picking, strumming, first chords, keeping a beat, and more! Plenty of photographs and diagrams are included to make it easy for anyone to learn, regardless of musical background. The songs use "EASY" chords, which are chords modified for younger players. The course it outlined step-by-step for immediate success.

The lessons can also be easily modified for older students using the standard versions of the chords. Many of the songs will display both for learning flexibility. There is also a handy chord chart at the back of the book for reference and further study. Furthermore, we've compiled instructional videos for many of the lessons online so you can watch and follow along. Visit *justplay-music.com* to learn more.

Parents and Teachers

This book is designed for a parent or teacher to assist in the lessons. Please encourage repetition and review. It's important to know that every student learns at their own pace, and encouragement is the best way to support their learning.

How to Use this Book

This book is written in a step-by-step manner, with sections that build on previous lessons. Each section starts with an explanation of the idea, followed by a lesson. For the best learning experience, proceed through the book as outlined and take time to allow weekly practice on each task.

A Note on Practice

When learning a musical instrument, practicing regularly is the key to success. Try and practice every day, even if it's for just 10 minutes at a time.

If this isn't possible, aim for three to four days a week. Start by taking 10 minutes to review the previous lesson, and then when you are ready, move on to the next exercise. As time goes on, try to increase the practice time to 15 or 20 minutes each day.

Just remember, it's important take a break when you need to. Let your fingers rest if they get sore. And don't forget, have fun! That's all you need to become a guitar superstar!

Section 1: About the Guitar

Guitar Types

Guitars come in different shapes, styles, and sizes. Most commonly, there are electric guitars, acoustic steel-string guitars, and classical guitars- any of these will work for this course.

Electric Guitar   **Acoustic Guitar**   **Classical Guitar**

Audio/video available at www.justplay-music.com

Guitar Size

Choosing the right size guitar.

Guitars are available in different sizes for different age groups. Below is a chart that will help you match your child's age to the best guitar size. Keep in mind that these are only guidelines.

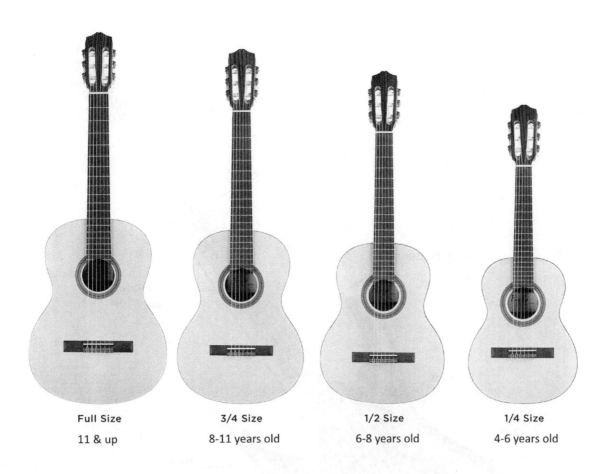

Full Size	3/4 Size	1/2 Size	1/4 Size
11 & up	8-11 years old	6-8 years old	4-6 years old

Parts of the Guitar

Even though there are different guitars, they all have standard features such as the head, tuners, nut, fretboard, and frets.

Electric Guitar

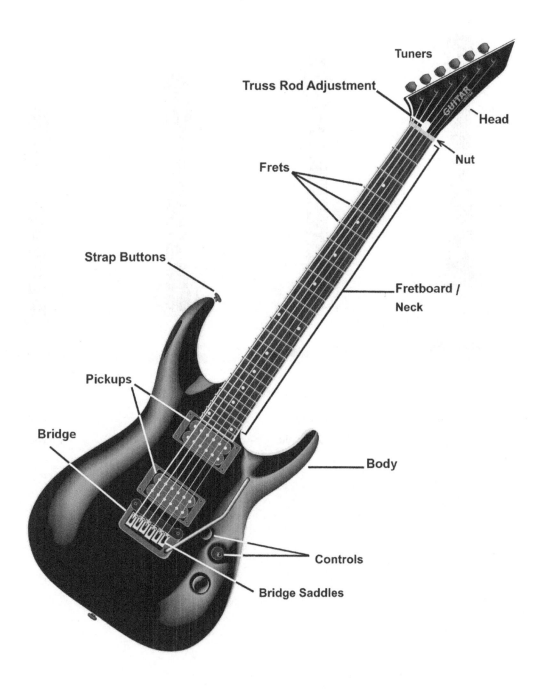

Acoustic Guitar

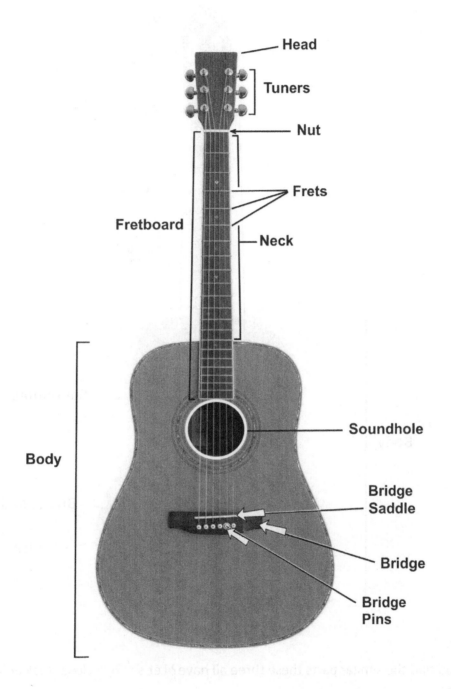

Head

Tuners

Nut

Frets

Fretboard

Neck

Body

Soundhole

Bridge
Saddle

Bridge

Bridge
Pins

Audio/video available at www.justplay-music.com

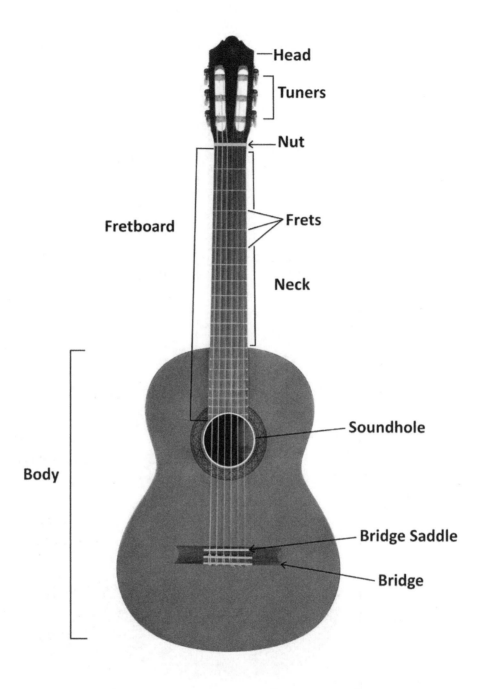

Did you find the similar parts these three all have? Let's take a closer look at key areas of the guitar.

The Fretboard

The fretboard is where we play the notes.

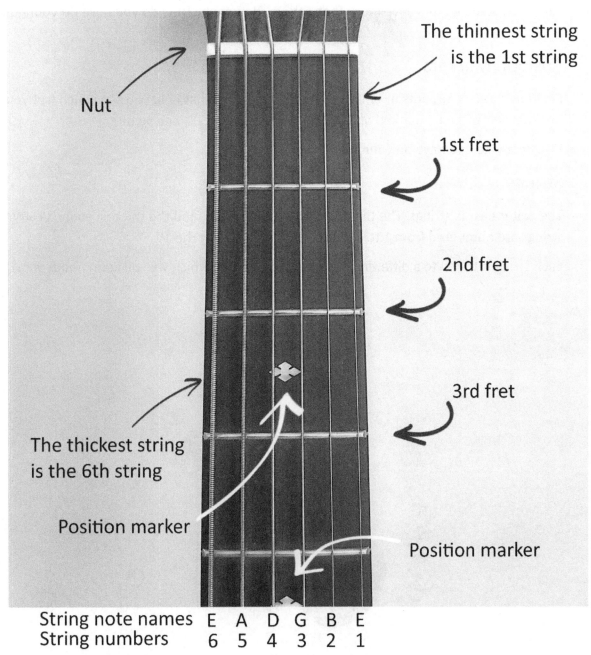

Nut

The thinnest string
is the 1st string

1st fret

2nd fret

3rd fret

The thickest string
is the 6th string

Position marker

Position marker

String note names	E	A	D	G	B	E
String numbers	6	5	4	3	2	1

Audio/video available at www.justplay-music.com

Frets

Frets are the metal bars on the fretboard. Starting at the 1st one closest to the nut, count each fret. Some guitars have more than others. How many frets do you have on your guitar?

Position Markers

Position markers are dots or emblems on the fretboard that help you see which fret you are on. They will often be marked on the 3rd, 5th, 7th, 9th, 12th, and so on.

How many do you have on your guitar?

Strings

The guitar has six strings. The thinnest string sound HIGH, and the thickest sounds LOW. The strings are numbered from 1 to 6, with the thinnest being the 1st.

Each string is tuned to a different musical note or pitch, which we will learn about shortly.

Audio/video available at www.justplay-music.com

Section 2: Playing Technique

Holding the Guitar

Begin by sitting up straight on a solid chair. When holding the guitar in a seated position, rest the arch of the guitar on your leg and hold it towards your chest. Drape your right arm over the top so that the forearm rests on the guitar's edge, just below your elbow. With your left hand, hold the neck to balance it.

NOTE: A music stand to hold your music at eye level will help with posture and concentration.

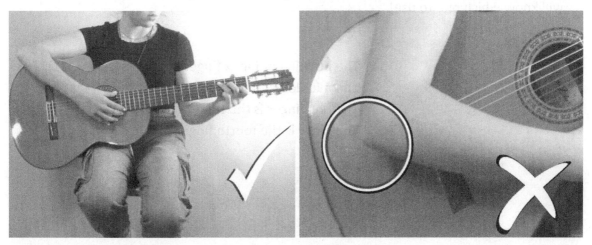

Be careful not to hang your whole arm over the guitar.

Left-Handed Players

Are you left-handed? Do you write with your left hand? If you're a "lefty," you can still try playing the guitar like a "righty." For many beginners, it makes no difference which way they start! Try both ways and see if there is much of a difference. If you feel better playing it left-handed, you can always find a left-handed guitar at the guitar store to try out. Depending on your guitar model, you may have it re-strung as left-handed at your local guitar store. When following the lessons in this book, simply reverse the references from right to left.

Audio/video available at www.justplay-music.com

Hand Positions

Left-Hand Position (Fretting Hand)

Finger Numbers

Certain fingers should be used when playing specific notes. To make this explanation very easy, number your fingers #1, #2, #3, and #4- starting with our pointing finger as #1 and ending with our pinky as #4. When you see instructions that say to use your #1 finger, you will know which one to use!

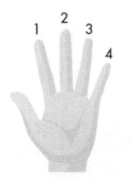

The pointing or index finger is the first finger (#1),
The middle finger is the 2nd finger (#2),
The ring finger is the third finger (#3),
The pinky is the fourth finger (#4).

Left hand finger numbers

The fingers of your fretting hand will push down on the strings in-between the frets. This is called "fretting" a note.

Press down on the strings using the very tip of your fingers and keep your thumb pressing on the back of the neck. This will be like 'pinching' the neck between your thumb and finger.

An easy explanation is to think of it as holding a hamburger between your thumb and fingers. The fingers are on the top, while the thumb is on the back.

14

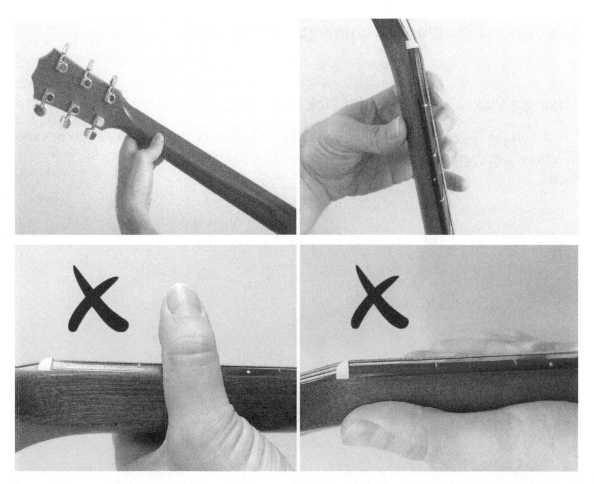

Try not to wrap your thumb around the neck or collapse your hand, so the thumb lays flat. These are common mistakes.

Right-Hand Position (Strumming/ Picking Hand)

Using a Pick: How to Hold a Pick

First, curl the fingers of your picking hand as pictured. Place the pick, so it sticks out about halfway. Lastly, grip the pick firmly with your thumb and hold it securely.

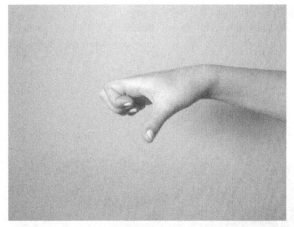

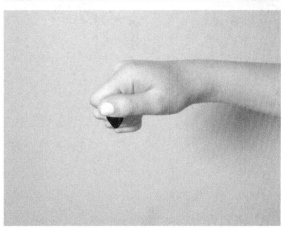

Picking Technique

Hold the pick securely but not too tight. Remember to stay relaxed. The pick should strike the string (s) straight down "towards the ground." Try picking one open string at a time, allowing it to come to a rest before the following string. If you don't have a pick, you can just use your thumb.

TIP: Try to avoid picking the string "outward" and away from the guitar (or inwards) as it will snap back against the frets and cause buzz and rattle.

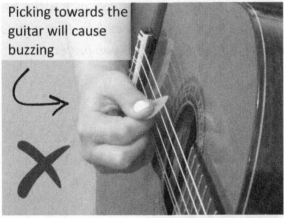

Picking towards the guitar will cause buzzing

Picking away from the guitar will cause buzzing

Strumming

Strumming is playing across the strings in a downward or upward motion. Try strumming all six strings downwards with the pick and see how it feels (playing the open strings)! Keep your hand relaxed and allow the pick to glide across the strings.

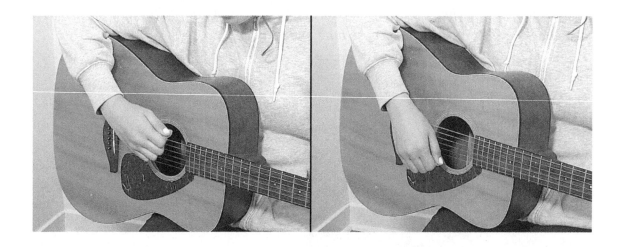

TIP: Picks come in different thicknesses and materials. A medium or soft pick is the best to start with as a beginner. Common materials such as Tortex, Nylon, or celluloid are all fine. It's good to try different picks initially, test them out, and see which ones you prefer.

Tuning

Now that you know how to hold your instrument and use a pick let's learn how to "tune" the guitar! The guitar needs to be tuned before it's played. It is normal to check and tune the guitar often.

The pitch or the string's note can be changed using the "tuning pegs." Turning the pegs tighter will sharpen the note, and the pitch will go higher. Loosening the pegs will flatten the note, and the pitch will lower. The standard tuning for the guitar strings from thick to thin is EADGBE. These are the notes that you will tune the strings to.

You can make a rhyme to remember the string notes, such as:

Eddy Ate Dynamite Good Bye Eddie

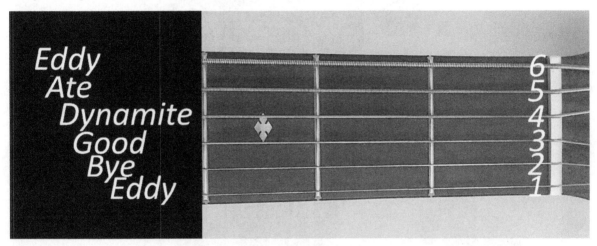

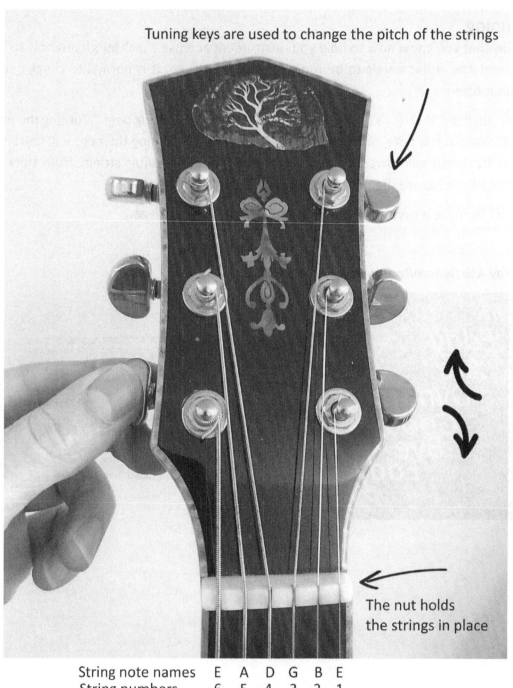

Tuning keys are used to change the pitch of the strings

The nut holds
the strings in place

String note names	E	A	D	G	B	E
String numbers	6	5	4	3	2	1

The most common way to tune a guitar is by using an electronic tuner or app on your smartphone. These devices will listen and show how "in-tune" you are by displaying a scale of each note. When you pluck the open string, it will show how "flat," "in-tune," or "sharp" you are to the note. The guitar won't sound very good unless it's tuned. Learning how to tune is an essential part of playing guitar.

How to Tune the Guitar

Hold the tuner close to the strings or attach it to the headstock if you have a clip-on.

Starting at the low E, or 6th string, pluck the string and check the tuner's display. Try to pluck the string at a medium force (not too hard or light). You will see the tuner respond as it listens to the note.

The display should read the note, showing E and how close to "in-tune" it is (see the example in the pictures below). If the note is too low (or flat), you might see a D or D# on the tuner. You will need to tighten the string until you see the E appear on display. You may see an F or F# if the note is too high. This means you need to loosen the string until it displays E.

Pluck the string again and turn the tuning peg until it's more in tune. Continue this until the display shows "in-tune." When done, move on to the next string.

The graphic below shows the range and order of musical notes you may come across while tuning.

NOTE: Musical notes are like the English alphabet, except they go only from A to G, then start over at A (repeating). So if you are tuning the Low E string and the tuner shows a D, you will need to tune up until it shows an E.

TIP: If you find the tuner keeps jumping around, keep plucking the string every couple of seconds to keep the note sounding steady. The tuner will respond with a steadier reading, making it easier for you to see.

Audio/video available at www.justplay-music.com

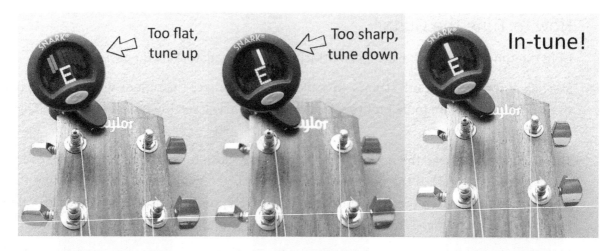

Too flat, tune up

Too sharp, tune down

In-tune!

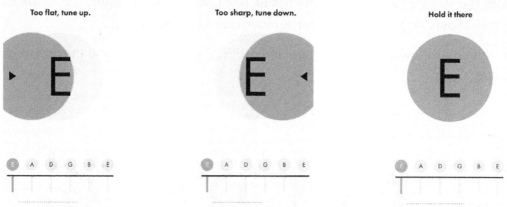

Too flat, tune up.

Too sharp, tune down.

Hold it there

Audio/video available at www.justplay-music.com

Tuning Tips

If you have any trouble, such as the string sounding too high or low, try to find an audible reference, such as going online and searching "guitar tuning reference." Often you can find this on YouTube or a similar website. Sometimes the string may get too far off the original pitch for a beginner to know where to tune to. Hearing a note reference may help you get the string back into closer range.

NOTE: If all the strings require a lot of tuning, you may need to go back and retune them all. The reason is that the change of string tension on the neck can affect the other strings, and sometimes a second check is required.

TIP: For best results, always tune "up" to the note, not "down." If you need to lower the note, tune "down" past the note and back "up." This way, the string won't slip out of tune as easily and will stay in tune much longer.

Remember, you must check and tune your guitar each time you pick it up for practice. Playing an out-of-tune guitar will not sound very good, no matter how hard you try.

Section 3: Let's Play!

Music Notation / Tablature (TAB) explained

For this next section, we will use a form of notation to best explain the single note picking exercises and songs. It's called Tablature.

Tablature is a chart made just for instruments like the guitar. It is read from left to right. The lines on the page symbolize the guitar strings and the numbers show us which fret to play on each string.

Tablature Explained

Tablature has 6 lines representing the 6 guitar strings.
The top line represents the <u>1st string</u> (the thinnest string).

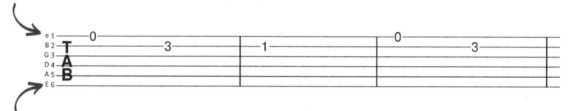

The bottom line represents the <u>6th string</u> (the thickest string).

The numbers show which frets to play on the corresponding strings.
Zero means to play the open string without fretting any notes.

0 means to play the "<u>open string</u>"(unfretted).

This means to play the <u>3rd fret</u> on the <u>2nd string</u>.

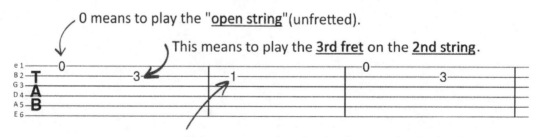

This mean to play the <u>1st fret</u> on the <u>2nd string</u>.

Audio/video available at www.justplay-music.com

Keeping the Beat

The "beat" of a song is the steady pulse behind it. It is the basic unit of time in music. It is the thing that makes our feet tap, and our heads bob when we are listening along.

The speed we play at is called the tempo. We can change the tempo of the beat, but the beat always remains the same. In our lessons, we will mostly count the beat in fours: 1, 2, 3, 4, and so on. But some other songs and lessons may count in threes, twos, sixes, or something else altogether!

We will always try to play with a steady beat for every lesson and song. A beat should stay steady like a clock. 1, 2, 3, 4. We can count aloud together. A parent or teacher can help by counting aloud while the student plays the notes. Try your best not to speed up or slow down! You can tap your foot at the same time to help.

Another way to help with keeping the best is to use a metronome. A metronome is a device that clicks like a clock but allows you to change the speed. These can also be found as a smartphone app. We can choose any tempo that works best for us and the lesson. Start slow, and you can increase the speed when you're ready.

Picking Exercise 1

First, we will start with an "open string" exercise and then integrate the fretting hand. "Open string" means to play the string without fretting down any notes.

Referring to the notation below, pick the 1st string (the thinnest string closest to the ground) four times. Pick down towards the ground at a right angle to the string.

In the next section, pick the 2nd string (the next string up from the 1st string) four times, being careful only to pick the 2nd string. Your pick should come to rest gently before the 1st string below.

Now alternate between picking the 1st string two times and picking the 2nd string two times.

You can end the exercise by picking the 1st string four last times.

Once you are comfortable with each section, try picking the entire piece of music to a steady beat.

Picking Exercise #1

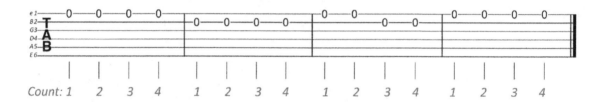

TIP: While doing these exercises, start slow and take your time. Allow each note to ring out until you play the following note.

You ROCK!!

Fretting Single Notes

Now we'll try fretting notes. Your fingers might get a little sore when you first start because they are not used to pressing down on the strings! But don't worry, it will get more comfortable as time goes on.

When fretting a note, place your finger just before the fret or in-between the frets, but not ON the frets. Let's play the 3rd fret on the 1st (skinniest) string, using our 3rd finger. See the following examples below.

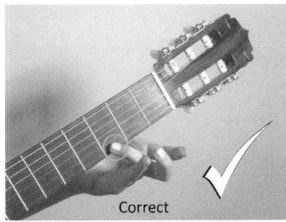

Correct

If you push down too hard, your finger will get tired fast, and the note may sound sharp. If you don't push hard enough, you will hear a buzzing sound. Try to experiment and listen to the results. The goal is to make the note sound and ring out clearly.

Too close to the fret

Too far from the fret

Audio/video available at www.justplay-music.com

Picking Exercise 2

In this next exercise, you will play a little song while learning to fret notes. Play each note and allow it to ring out until you play the following note. Try this throughout the exercise.

But Which Finger Do We Use?

This is a good question and an important topic. In this exercise, you can use the same fingers as the fret notes. So, when you see the 1st fret, use your 1st finger. When you see the 3rd fret, use your 3rd finger. I've added the pictures below for you to see what I mean.

Picking Exercise #2

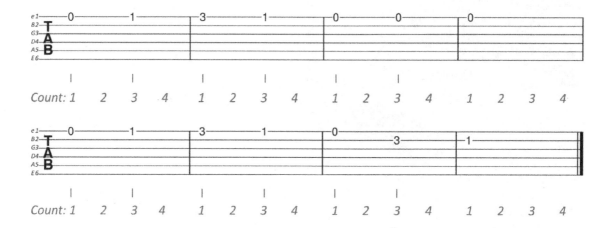

28

Audio/video available at www.justplay-music.com

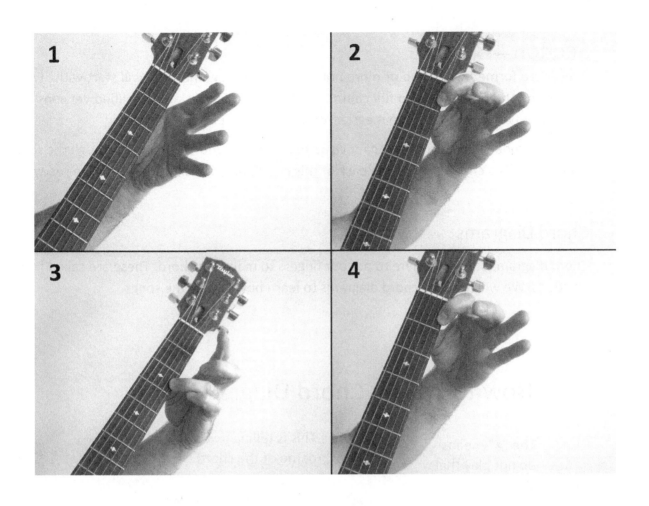

And for the last two notes on the 2nd string.

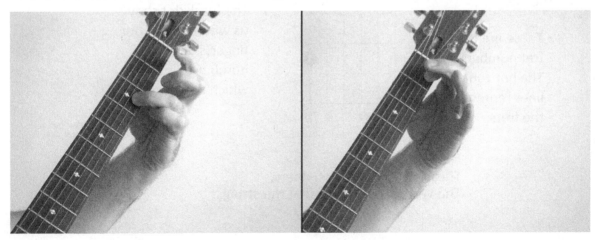

Section 4: Chords

Chords are formed when two or more notes are played together. We will start with "EASY" chords and then progress into full chords. "EASY" guitar chords are simplified versions that use one or two fingers- to make it easier for beginners, especially children.

Once the student is ready, they can move up to the "FULL" chords and play through the songs again. There is a chord chart at the back of this book that you can use once you're ready.

Chord Diagrams

Chord diagrams show us where to put our fingers to make the chord. These are called finger positions. We will read the chord diagrams to learn how to play the songs.

How to Read a Chord Diagram

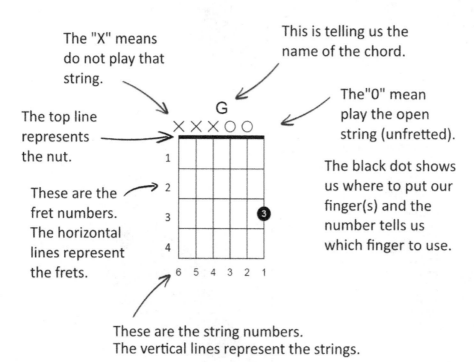

This tells us to place our 3rd finger on the 3rd fret of the 1st string and to play/strum the 3rd, 2nd, and 1st strings only.

30

The G Chord

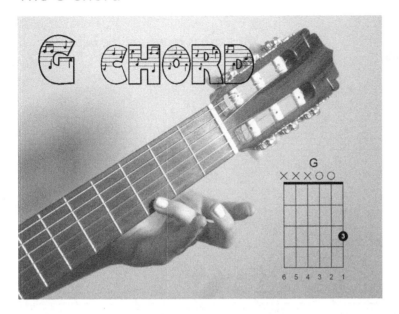

Using your 3rd finger, fret the 3rd fret on the 1st string. Then gently strum the strings from the 3rd downward to the 1st. Let's try it out now!

So, how does it sound? After strumming the chord, try picking each string individually, from the 3rd string down to the 1st. Each string of the chord should ring out clearly. Once you can hear that, you did it!

Strumming Exercise 1

Strumming exercises help with coordination and rhythm. You can run through them one at a time while a parent or teacher counts aloud. The following exercises can be practiced separately or one after another.

Begin by slowly counting out loud from one to four repeatedly: 1, 2, 3, 4, 1, 2, 3, 4 and so on.

EXERCISE 1.0 (strum on the count of one): Strum the chord at the count of one and let it ring out until you return to one again. Strum again and make sure it rings out full for the count from one to four.

EXERCISE 1.1 (strum on the count of one and two): This time, strum at the count of one and two while allowing the chord to ring out afterwards until you return to the next count of one and two.

EXERCISE 1.2 (strum on the count of one and three): Strum the chord every time you count one and three. Let the chord ring out in-between strums.

EXERCISE 1.3 (strum on every beat): Strum on every beat for the last exercise.

Audio/video available at www.justplay-music.com

Exercise 1.0
Strum on the count of one.

The slashes represent the beat.

Exercise 1.1
Strum on the count of one and two.

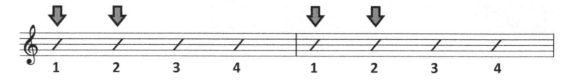

Exercise 1.2
Strum on the count of one and three.

Exercise 1.3
Strum on every beat.

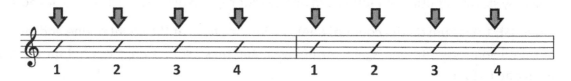

GREAT JOB!!

Audio/video available at www.justplay-music.com

The C Chord

The "C" chord is tricky as there are two open strings to be played alongside the fretted note. This can only be achieved by arching your finger to avoid muting the other strings. Press down the 1st fret of the 2nd string, using the tip of your 1st finger. Strum the strings shown, from the 3rd down to the 1st.

When first learning this chord, be careful not to mute the 1st by your finger. If this happens, arch your finger up a little more.

TIP: Once you have fretted the note, pick each string of the chord individually. Pick down from the 3rd string to the 1st to make sure they all ring out.

It may take a few practices until you get it, as some chords will be more challenging than others. Just remember to be patient and have fun with it!

Audio/video available at www.justplay-music.com

Changing Chords

Once you've learned your first two chords, the next lesson is to learn how to change from one to the other. First, place your 3rd finger on the 3rd fret of the 1st string to make a G chord. Strum and then relax. Then place your 1st finger on the 1st fret of the 2nd string to make the C chord and strum again. Repeat this exercise a few times over when you are ready.

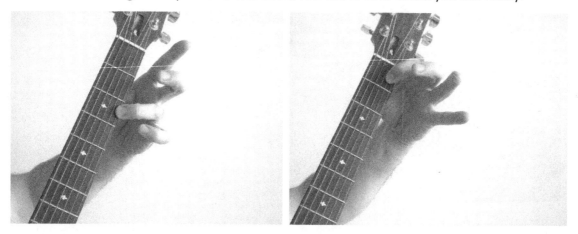

There are several songs that you can play using these two chords alone! Take your time with it and practice until it gets easy. Here are some strumming exercises to help with timing and coordination.

Strumming Exercise 2

EXERCISE 2.0 (strum on the count of one): This is like the exercise you did when you strummed the G chord on the count of one. However, this time you will change to the C chord after you reach the count of four. At first, it will take a moment to adjust your fingers, and you may need to pause your counting.

EXERCISE 2.1 (strum on the count of one and two): This time, you will strum the G chord on the count of one and two and then change to the C chord for the following count of one and two.

EXERCISE 2.2 (strum on the count of one and three): Strum the G chord at the count of one and three, then change to the C chord for the next count of one and three.

EXERCISE 2.3 (strum on every beat): For the last exercise, strum the G chord on every beat as you count 1, 2, 3, 4, and then change to the C chord and do the same.

This exercise will take some time and practice until it feels natural, so start slow and gradually increase speed when you're comfortable. Remember to try your best to make the chords ring out for the entire count from one to four.

Exercise 2.0
Strum on the count of one.
The "C" shows when to change the chord.

The slashes represent the beat.
You can repeat the line several times.

Exercise 2.1
Strum on the count of one and two.

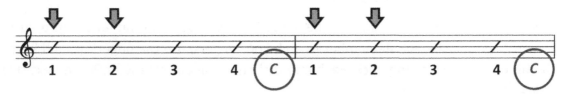

Exercise 2.2
Strum on the count of one and three.

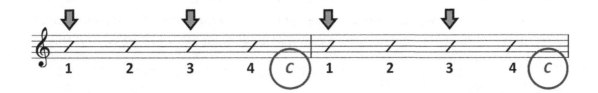

Exercise 2.3
Strum on every beat.

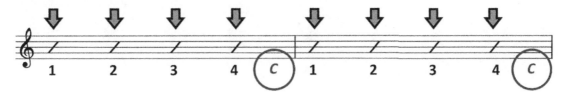

35

Section 5: Songs

Now that we have covered all the fundamentals, we are ready to learn songs. So far, we have learned all about proper playing technique, hand positions, how to use a pick, tune, read chord charts, finger placement, pick control, and strumming! Ready to play some songs?

How to Practice Songs

We will start every song by counting out loud slowly, just like before. This will be our beat to play along to. It's usually best to start counting slow and later increase the tempo (speed) once we've learned the chord changes. Another way to help with this is to use a metronome. We can choose any tempo that works best for us, the lesson, and the song. If it feels too rushed, slow it down.

Before starting, be familiar with the song. This will help the lesson overall and be more enjoyable for the student while they strum along. This is where the parent or teacher can help by singing along to the music. Once the student has learnt the strumming, they can feel free to join the fun and sing along too!

Practice the chords before starting the song. Take as much time on each chord, including proper finger placement. Remember to arch your fingers, use the fingertips, and keep your thumb on the back of the neck. Each chord should ring out clearly until the next strum is indicated.

Each song will have a suggestion as to when to strum the strings. The examples have been given for the beginner to learn coordination and rhythm. Once they have learnt the suggested strumming pattern for the song, they can try a different pattern that may be more challenging. Referring to our examples in our Exercises, any of these can be applied or expanded upon on (*see additional exercises at the end of the book*). The student can continue developing their strumming into more complexity as their skills progress, and this can be a lot of fun!

Are you ready?!

SONG

Strum the chord when you see it above the lyrics. See the next page for a new strumming example and a lyric-focused visual example.

G

The slash lines represent the beat as we count 1, 2, 3, 4, and so on.
To start, strum on every count of one. Have a parent or teacher count and sing along while you play.

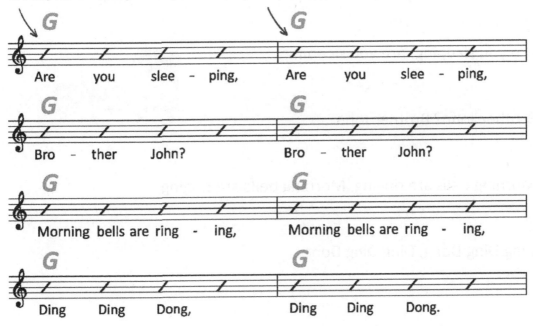

Audio/video available at www.justplay-music.com

Once you've got the hang of it, you can expand on this
lesson and strum on the count of one and three.

G *G* *G* *G*

Are   you   slee - ping,   Are   you   slee - ping,

G *G* *G* *G*

Bro - ther   John?   Bro - ther   John?

G *G* *G* *G*

Morning bells are ring - ing,   Morning bells are ring - ing,

G *G* *G* *G*

Ding   Ding   Dong,   Ding   Ding   Dong.

The following is another way we may see the chords displayed throughout this lesson book.

G   *G*   *G*   *G*

Are you sleeping, Are you sleeping?

G   *G*   *G*   *G*

Brother John? Brother John?

G   *G*   *G*   *G*

Morning bells are ringing, Morning bells are ringing,

G   *G*   *G*   *G*

Ding Ding Dong, Ding Ding Dong.

38

SONG

Row, Row, Row Your Boat

With chord change. In this song we will learn how to change from the C chord to the G chord and back again.

SONG

MARY HAD A LITTLE LAMB

This song will have us changing chords on every line. See the next page for additional (optional) verses.

C	C	G	C

Mary   had   a   little   lamb,   Little   lamb,   little   lamb.

C	C	G	C

Mary   had   a   little   lamb,   It's fleece was white as snow.

C	C	G	C

Every - where that Mary   went,   Mary   went,   Mary   went.

C	C	G	C

Every - where that Mary   went,   The lamb was sure to go.

Audio/video available at www.justplay-music.com

The following verses can be played using the same chords and rhythm.

C	C	G	C

It followed her to school one day, school one day, school one day,

It followed her to school one day, which was against the rules.

It made the children laugh and play, laugh and play, laugh and play,

it made the children laugh and play, to see a lamb at school.

And so the teacher turned it out, turned it out, turned it out,

And so the teacher turned it out, but still it lingered near.

And waited patiently about, patiently about, patiently about,

And waited patiently about, till Mary did appear.

"Why does the lamb love Mary so?" Love Mary so? Love Mary so?

"Why does the lamb love Mary so," the eager children cry.

"Why, Mary loves the lamb, you know." The lamb, you know, the lamb, you know,

"Why, Mary loves the lamb, you know," the teacher did reply.

41

SONG

LONDON BRIDGE IS FALLING DOWN

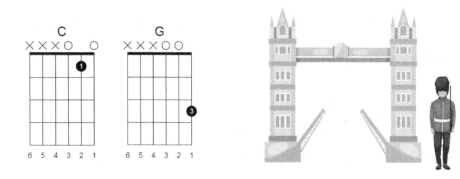

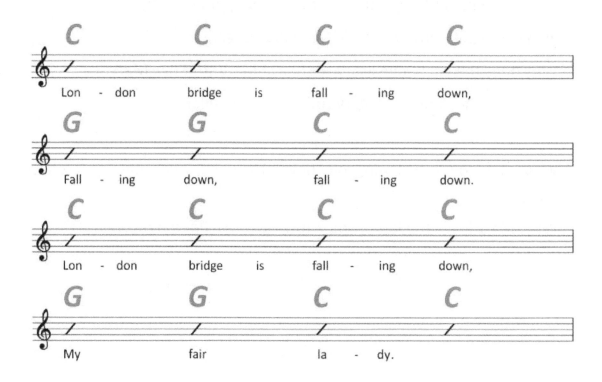

C   C   C   C

Lon - don   bridge   is   fall - ing   down,

G   G   C   C

Fall - ing   down,   fall - ing   down.

C   C   C   C

Lon - don   bridge   is   fall - ing   down,

G   G   C   C

My   fair   la - dy.

42

The G7 Chord

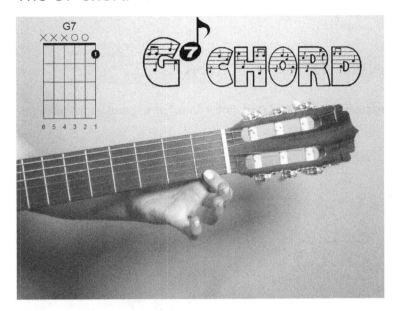

The next chord we will learn is G7. It's similar to G but instead of playing the 3rd fret, we play the 1st.

Using your 1st finger, fret the 1st fret on the 1st string. Then gently strum the strings from the 3rd downward to the 1st. Let's try it out now!

43

SONG

Rain, Rain, Go Away

In this song, we'll practice going from the chord of C to a new chord of G7, and back again.

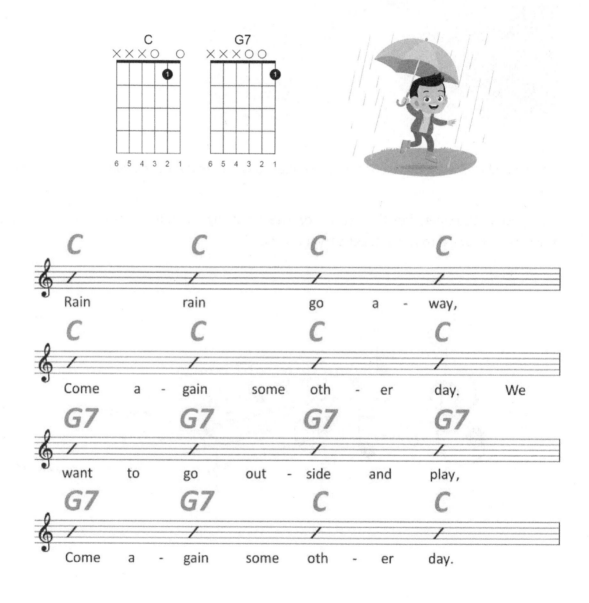

C   C   C   C

Rain   rain   go   a - way,

C   C   C   C

Come   a - gain   some   oth - er   day.   We

G7   G7   G7   G7

want   to   go   out - side   and   play,

G7   G7   C   C

Come   a - gain   some   oth - er   day.

SONG

A TISKET, A TASKET

For this song you can strum on every beat as noted above the lyrics. To expand on this lesson and try a new challenge, you can strum on every half beat as well (in between each beat). See Strumming Exercise 4.0 on page 86 for an example.

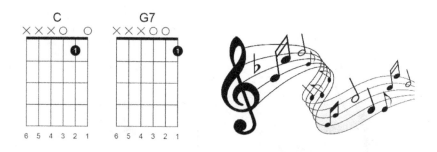

1, 2, 3, 4, "A..."

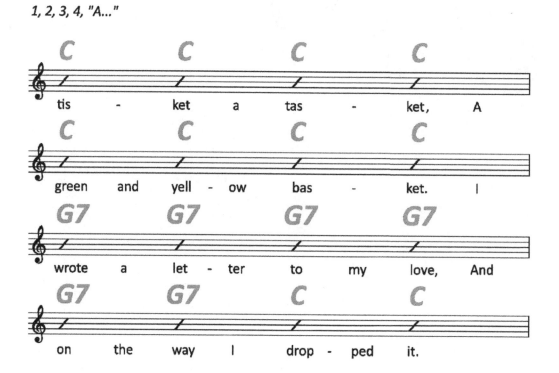

| C | C | C | C |
| tis - | ket | a | tas - | ket, | A |

| C | C | C | C |
| green | and | yell - | ow | bas - | ket. | I |

| G7 | G7 | G7 | G7 |
| wrote | a | let - | ter | to | my | love, | And |

| G7 | G7 | C | C |
| on | the | way | I | drop - | ped | it. |

The following verses can be played using the same chords and rhythm.

  C   *C* *C*   *C*

I dropped it, I dropped it,

   C   *C* *C*   *C*

and on the way I dropped it.

  G7 *G7* *G7* *G7*

A little girl, she picked it up,

   G7 *G7* *C* *C*

and put it in her po - cket.

   C *C*   *C* *C*

Her po-cket, her po-cket,

   C *C* *C* *C*

she put it in her po - cket.

  G7 *G7* *G7* *G7*

A little girl, she picked it up,

   G7 *G7* *C* *C*

and put it in her po - cket.

Audio/video available at www.justplay-music.com

SONG

HUSH LITTLE BABY

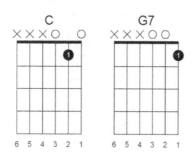

C		C		G7		G7	
Hush,	little	baby,		don't	say	a	word,

G7		G7		C		C	
Mama's	gonna	buy	you a	mock	-	ing	bird. And

C		C		G7		G7	
if	that	mock	-	ing	bird	won't	sing,

G7		G7		C		C	
Mama's	gonna	buy	you a	dia	-	mond	ring.

48

The following verses can be played using the same chords and rhythm.

    C   C   G7   G7

And if that diamond ring turns brass,

G7   G7   C   C

Mama's gonna buy you a looking glass.

    C   C   G7   G7

And if that looking glass gets broke,

G7   G7   C   C

Mama's gonna buy you a billy goat.

And if that billy goat won't pull,

Mama's gonna buy you a cart and bull.

And if that cart and bull turn over,

Mama's going to buy you a dog named Rover.

And if that dog named Rover won't bark,

Mama's going to buy you a horse and cart.

And if that horse and cart fall down,

You'll still be the sweetest little baby in town.

SONG

This Old Man

In this song, we will practice changing between the three chords C, G7 and G.

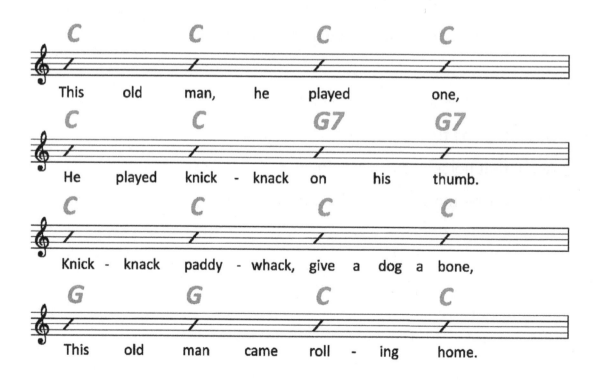

The following verses can be played using the same chords and rhythm.

This old man, he played two,

He played knick-knack on my shoe.

Knick-knack paddywhack,

Give a dog a bone,

This old man came rolling home.

This old man, he played three,

He played knick-knack on my knee.

Knick-knack paddywhack,

Give a dog a bone,

This old man came rolling home.

This old man, he played four,

He played knick-knack on my door.

Knick-knack paddywhack,

Give a dog a bone,

This old man came rolling home.

This old man, he played five,

He played knick-knack on my hive.

Knick-knack paddywhack,

Give a dog a bone,

This old man came rolling home.

This old man, he played six,

He played knick-knack on my sticks.

Knick-knack paddywhack,

Give a dog a bone,

This old man came rolling home.

This old man, he played seven,

He played knick-knack up in Heaven.

Knick-knack paddywhack,

Give a dog a bone,

This old man came rolling home.

This old man, he played eight,

He played knick-knack on my gate.

Knick-knack paddywhack,

Give a dog a bone,

This old man came rolling home.

This old man, he played nine,

He played knick-knack on my spine.

Knick-knack paddywhack,

Give a dog a bone,

This old man came rolling home.

This old man, he played ten,

He played knick-knack once again.

Knick-knack paddywhack,

Give a dog a bone,

This old man came rolling home

Audio/video available at www.justplay-music.com

The D7 Chord

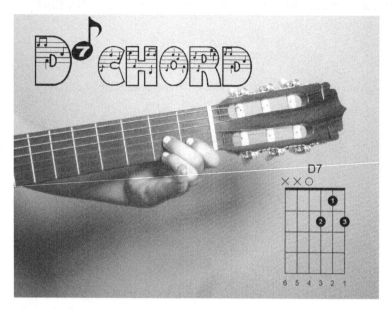

The next chord we will learn is D7. This time we will be fretting down three different notes to make the chord.

Using your 1st finger, fret the 1st fret on the 2nd string. Reach over with your 2nd finger and fret down the 2nd fret on the 3rd string. Now tuck your 3rd finger in and fret the 2nd fret on the 1st string. Then gently strum the strings from the 4th string downward to the 1st. Optionally, you can strum from the 3rd string down. Let's try it out now!

Once you've got the hang of it, we will move on to the next song.

SONG

THE WHEELS ON THE BUS

In this song we will learn to change from G to a new chord, D7.

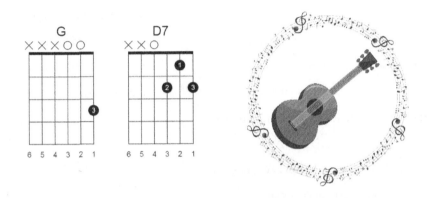

1, 2, 3, 4, "The..."

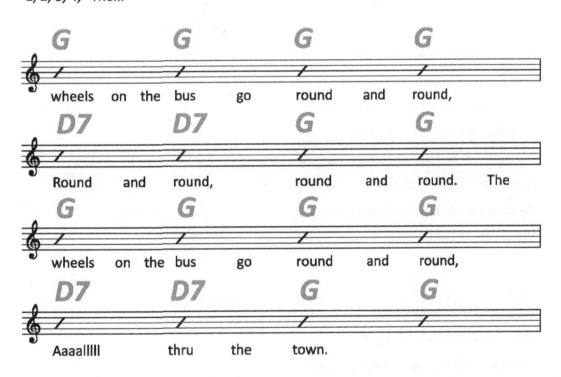

G	G	G	G

wheels   on   the   bus   go   round   and   round,

D7	D7	G	G

Round   and   round,   round   and   round.   The

G	G	G	G

wheels   on   the   bus   go   round   and   round,

D7	D7	G	G

Aaaalllll   thru   the   town.

The following verses can be played using the same chords and rhythm.

The wipers on the bus go "Swish, swish, swish,

Swish, swish, swish, swish, swish, swish"

The wipers on the bus go "Swish, swish, swish"

All through the town.

(*Make windshield wipers with arms*)

The door on the bus goes open and shut

Open and shut, open and shut

The door on the bus goes open and shut

All through the town. (*Cover eyes with hands*)

The horn on the bus goes "Beep, beep, beep

Beep, beep, beep, beep, beep, beep"

The horn on the bus goes "Beep, beep, beep"

All through the town. (*Honk horn*)

The gas on the bus goes "Glug, glug, glug

Glug, glug, glug, glug, glug, glug"

The gas on the bus goes "Glug, glug, glug"

All through the town. (*Fill gas tank*)

The money on the bus goes "Clink, clink, clink,

Clink, clink, clink, clink, clink, clink"

The money on the bus goes "Clink, clink, clink"

All through the town. (*Put money in cash box*)

The baby on the bus says, "Wah, wah, wah!

Wah, wah, wah, wah, wah, wah!"

The baby on the bus says, "Wah, wah, wah!"

All through the town. (*Hands in fists rub eyes*)

The people on the bus say, "Shh, shh, shh,

Shh, shh, shh, shh, shh, shh"

The people on the bus say, "Shh, shh, shh"

All through the town. (*Pointer finger to mouth*)

The mommy on the bus says, "I love you,

I love you, I love you"

The daddy on the bus says, "I love you, too"

All through the town. (*Hug yourself*)

Full Chords

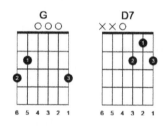

SONG

Itsy Bitsy Spider

In this song we will gain more practice changing between the G chord and D7 on every line.

1, 2, 3, 4, "The..."

G	G	D7	G

itsy - bitsy   spi - der   went   up   the   water   spout.

G	G	D7	G

Down   came   the   rain   and   washed the spider   out.

G	G	D7	G

Out   came   the   sun   and   dried up   all   the   rain.   So   the

G	G	D7	G

itsy - bitsy   spi - der   went   up   the   spout   again!

SONG

He's Got the Whole World in His Hands

After playing through this song as shown below, you can expand on the lesson by strumming on every half beat as well (in between each beat). See Strumming Exercise 4.0 on page 86 for an example.

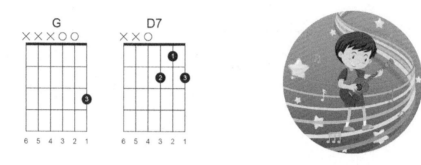

1, 2, 3, 4, "He's got the..."

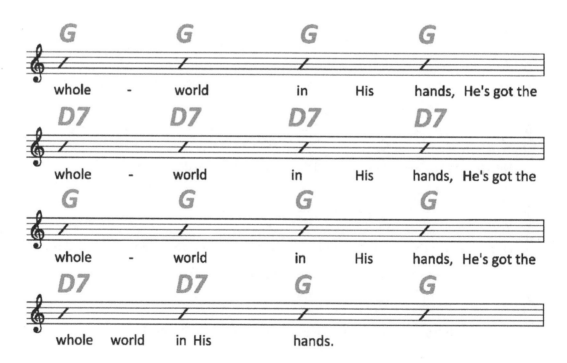

G   G   G   G

whole - world   in   His   hands, He's got the

D7   D7   D7   D7

whole - world   in   His   hands, He's got the

G   G   G   G

whole - world   in   His   hands, He's got the

D7   D7   G   G

whole   world   in His   hands.

The following verses can be played using the same chords and rhythm.

He's got the wind and the rain in His hands,

He's got the wind and the rain in His hands,

He's got the wind and the rain in His hands,

He's got the whole world in His hands.

He's got the sun and the moon in His hands,

He's got the sun and the moon in His hands,

He's got the sun and the moon in His hands,

He's got the whole world in His hands.

He's got the little bitty baby in His hands,

He's got the little bitty baby in His hands,

He's got the little bitty baby in His hands,

He's got the whole world in His hands.

He's got you and me Brother in His hands,

He's got you and me Brother in His hands,

He's got you and me Brother in His hands,

He's got the whole world in His hands.

He's got you and me Sister in His hands,

He's got you and me Sister in His hands,

He's got you and me Sister in His hands,

He's got the whole world in His hands.

He's got everybody here in His hands,

He's got everybody here in His hands,

He's got everybody here in His hands,

He's got the whole world in His hands.

Full Chords

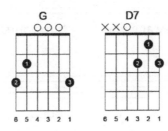

57

SONG

HOKEY POKEY

After playing through this song as shown below, you can also try strumming on every half beat as well (in between every beat).

1, 2, 3, 4, "You put your..."

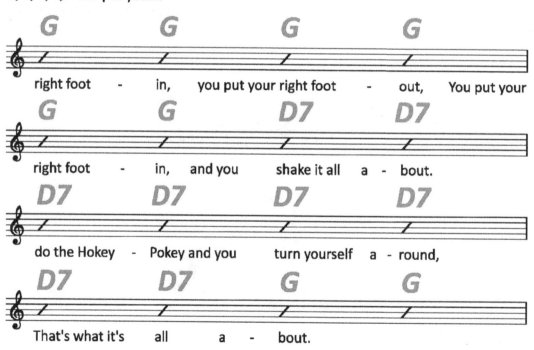

| G | G | G | G |
right foot - in, you put your right foot - out, You put your

| G | G | D7 | D7 |
right foot - in, and you shake it all a - bout.

| D7 | D7 | D7 | D7 |
do the Hokey - Pokey and you turn yourself a - round,

| D7 | D7 | G | G |
That's what it's all a - bout.

The following verses can be played using the sae chords and rhythm.

You put your left foot in,
You put your left foot out,
You put your left foot in,
And you shake it all about.
You do the Hokey Pokey
And you turn yourself around,
That's what it's all about.

You put your right hand in,
You put your right hand out,
You put your right hand in
And you shake it all about.
You do the Hokey Pokey
And you turn yourself around,
That's what it's all about.

You put your left hand in,
You put your left hand out,
You put your left hand in,
And you shake it all about.
You do the Hokey Pokey
And you turn yourself around,
That's what it's all about.

You put your right shoulder in,
You put your right shoulder out,
You put your right shoulder in,
And you shake it all about.
You do the Hokey Pokey
And you turn yourself around,
That's what it's all about.

You put your left shoulder in,
You put your left shoulder out,
You put your left shoulder in,
And you shake it all about.
You do the Hokey Pokey
And you turn yourself around,
That's what it's all about.

You put your right hip in,
You put your right hip out,
You put your right hip in
And you shake it all about.
You do the Hokey Pokey
And you turn yourself around,
That's what it's all about.

You put your left hip in,
You put your left hip out,
You put your left hip in,
And you shake it all about.
You do the Hokey Pokey
And you turn yourself around,
That's what it's all about.

You put your whole self in,
You put your whole self out,
You put your whole self in
And you shake it all about.
You do the Hokey Pokey
And you turn yourself around,
That's what it's all about.

Audio/video available at www.justplay-music.com

SONG

SHE'LL BE COMING 'ROUND THE MOUNTAIN

In this song, we will practice changing between three chords including G, C, and D7. To make it more challenging, you can also strum in between every beat (every half-beat).

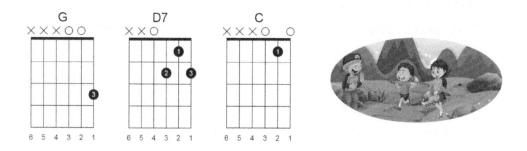

1, 2, 3, 4, "She'll be..."

| G | G | G | G |

coming   round the mountain when she comes, (when she comes!)   She'll be

| G | G | D7 | D7 |

coming   round the mountain when she comes, (when she comes!)   She'll be

| G | G | C | C |

coming round the   mountain, She'll be coming round the   mountain, She'll be

| G | D7 | G | G |

coming round the   mountain when she comes. (when she comes!)

The following verses can be played using the same chords and rhythm.

She'll be driving six white horses when she comes, (when she comes!)

She'll be driving six white horses when she comes, (when she comes!)

She'll be driving six white horses,

She'll be driving six white horses,

She'll be driving six white horses when she comes. (when she comes!)

Oh, we'll all go out to meet her when she comes, (when she comes!)

Oh, we'll all go out to meet her when she comes, (when she comes!)

Oh, we'll all go out to meet her,

We'll all go out to meet her,

We'll all go out to meet her when she comes. (when she comes!)

We'll be havin' chicken and dumplings when she comes, (when she comes!)

We'll be havin' chicken and dumplings when she comes, (when she comes!)

We'll be havin' chicken and dumplings,

We'll be havin' chicken and dumplings,

We'll be havin' chicken and dumplings when she comes. (when she comes!)

Full Chords

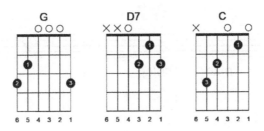

SONG

WHEN THE SAINTS GO MARCHING IN

The strumming pattern can be played on every beat of 1, 2, 3, 4. To expand on this lesson and try a new challenge, you can strum on every half beat as well. See Strumming Exercise 4.1 on page 86 for a mixed "down-up-down" strumming example.

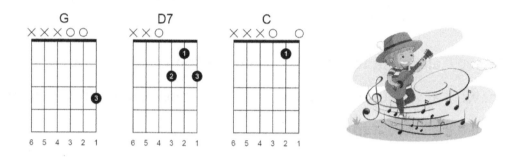

1, 2, 3, "Oh, when the..."

The following verses can be played using the same chords and rhythm.

And when the sun begins to shine,

And when the sun begins to shine,

Lord, how I want to be in that number,

When the sun begins to shine.

Oh, when the trumpet sounds its call,

Oh, when the trumpet sounds its call,

Lord, how I want to be in that number,

When the trumpet sounds its call.

Some say this world of trouble,

Is the only one we need,

But I'm waiting for that morning,

When the new world is revealed.

Full Chords

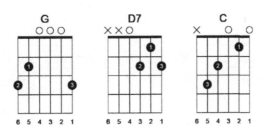

SONG

HAPPY BIRTHDAY TO YOU

This song we will count in three's: 1, 2, 3, 1, 2, 3, and so on.

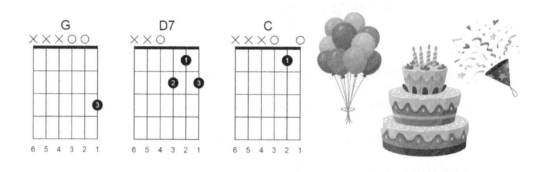

(Optional: "and many more....")

Full Chords

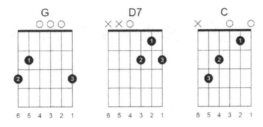

65

SONG

If You're Happy and You Know It

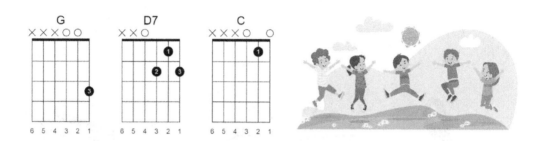

1, 2, 3, 4 "If you're..."

| G | G | D7 | D7 |

Happy and you know it clap your hands, (clap) (clap) If you're

| D7 | D7 | G | G |

happy and you know it clap your hands. (clap) (clap) If you're

| C | C | G | G |

happy and you know it, then your face will surely show it, If you're

| D7 | D7 | G | G |

happy and you know it clap your hands. (clap) (clap)

Audio/video available at www.justplay-music.com

The following verses can be played using he same chords and rhythm.

If you're happy and you know it, tap your toe. (Tap twice)

If you're happy and you know it, tap your toe. (Tap twice)

If you're happy and you know it, then your face will surely show it,

If you're happy and you know it, tap your toe. (Tap twice)

If you're happy and you know it, nod your head. (Nod head)

If you're happy and you know it, nod your head. (Nod head)

If you're happy and you know it, then your face will surely show it,

If you're happy and you know it, nod your head. (Nod head)

If you're happy and you know it, clap your hands. (Clap twice)

If you're happy and you know it, clap your hands. (Clap twice)

If you're happy and you know it, then your face will surely show it,

If you're happy and you know it, clap your hands. (Clap twice)

Full Chords

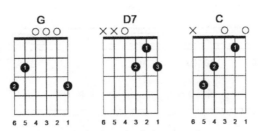

Audio/video available at www.justplay-music.com

SONG

 OLD MACDONALD HAD A FARM

In this song, there are plenty of chord changes between G, C, and D7. After playing through as shown below, you can to try a new challenge by incorporating different strumming examples such as strumming every half beat as well. See Strumming Exercise 4.1 on page 86 for a mixed "down-up-down" strumming example.

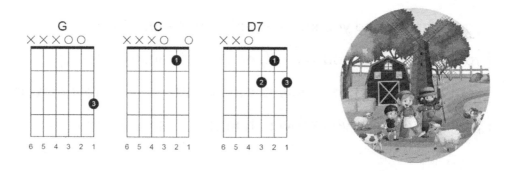

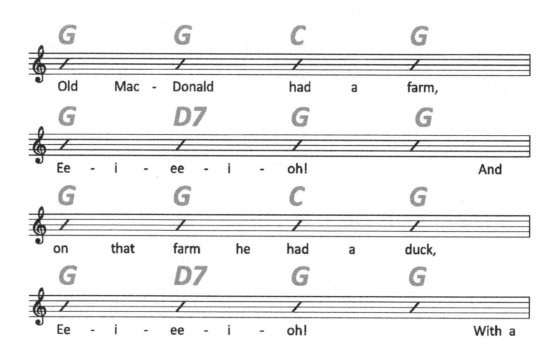

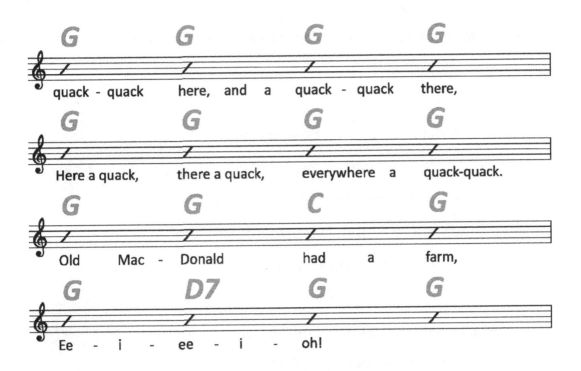

G	G	G	G

quack - quack   here,   and   a   quack - quack   there,

G	G	G	G

Here a quack,   there a quack,   everywhere a   quack-quack.

G	G	C	G

Old   Mac - Donald   had   a   farm,

G	D7	G	G

Ee   -   i   -   ee - i -   oh!

69

The following verses can be played using he same chords and rhythm.

Old MacDonald had a farm, Ee-i-ee-i-oh!

And on that farm he had a cow, Ee-i-ee-i-oh!

With a moo-moo here, And a moo-moo there

Here a moo, there a moo, Everywhere a moo-moo

Old MacDonald had a farm Ee-i-ee-i-oh!

Old MacDonald had a farm, Ee-i-ee-i-oh!

And on that farm he had a pig, Ee-i-ee-i-oh!

With an oink-oink here, And an oink-oink there,

Here an oink, there an oink, Everywhere an oink-oink.

Old MacDonald had a farm Ee-i-ee-i-oh!

Old MacDonald had a farm, Ee-i-ee-i-oh!

And on that farm he had a horse, Ee-i-ee-i-oh!

With a neigh-neigh here, And a neigh-neigh there

Here a neigh, there a neigh, Everywhere a neigh-neigh.

Old MacDonald had a farm, Ee-i-ee-i-oh!

Full Chords

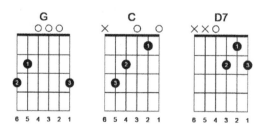

70

SONG

TWINKLE TWINKLE LITTLE STAR / THE ALPHABET SONG

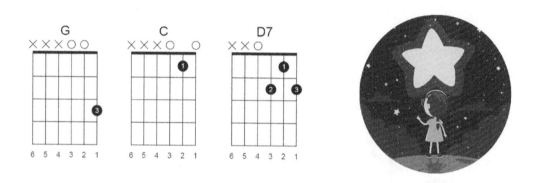

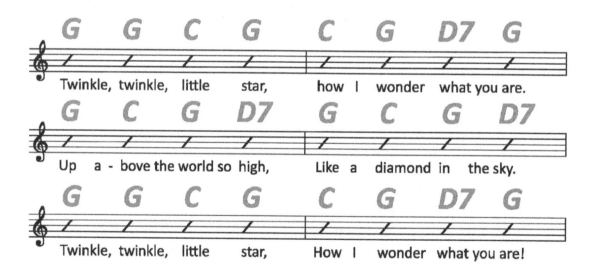

| G | | G | | C | | G | | | C | | G | | D7 | | G |

Twinkle, twinkle, little star, how I wonder what you are.

| G | | C | | G | | D7 | | G | | C | | G | | D7 |

Up a - bove the world so high, Like a diamond in the sky.

| G | | G | | C | | G | | | C | | G | | D7 | | G |

Twinkle, twinkle, little star, How I wonder what you are!

The following verses can be played using he same chords and rhythm.

When the blazing sun is gone,

When he nothing shines upon,

Then you show your little light,

Twinkle, twinkle, all the night.

Twinkle, twinkle, little star,

How I wonder what you are!

Then the traveler in the dark

Thanks you for your tiny spark;

He could not see which way to go,

If you did not twinkle so.

Twinkle, twinkle, little star,

How I wonder what you are!

Full Chords

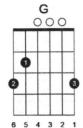
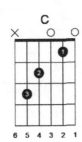

SONG

YOU ARE MY SUNSHINE ☀

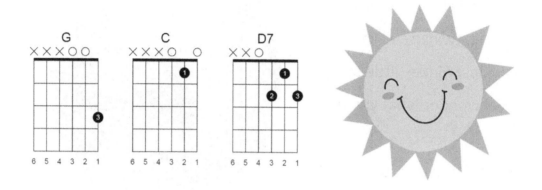

1, 2, 3, "You..."

are my sun - shine, my only sun - shine. You

make me hap - py when skies are grey. You'll

never know, dear, how much I love you.

Please don't take my sun - shine a - way.

74

Full Chords

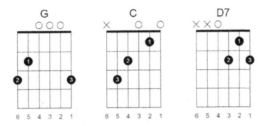

The D Chord

The next chord we will learn is D. It's similar to D7 but we have to reposition our fingers to play it.

Using your 1st finger, fret the 2nd fret on the 3rd string. Then use your 2nd finger and fret down the 2nd fret on the 1st string. Now reach over with your 3rd finger and fret the 3rd fret on the 2nd string. Then gently strum the strings from the 4th string downward to the 1st. Optionally, you can strum from the 3rd string down. Let's try it out now!

SONG

DOWN BY THE BAY

The strumming pattern can be played on every beat of 1, 2, 3, 4. To expand on this lesson and try a new challenge, you can strum on every half beat as well. See Strumming Exercise 4.2 on page 86 for a mixed "down-up-down" strumming example.

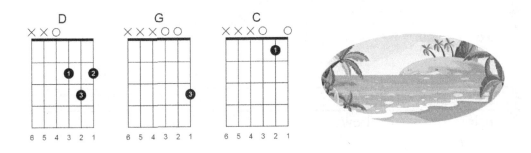

1, 2, 3, "Down..."

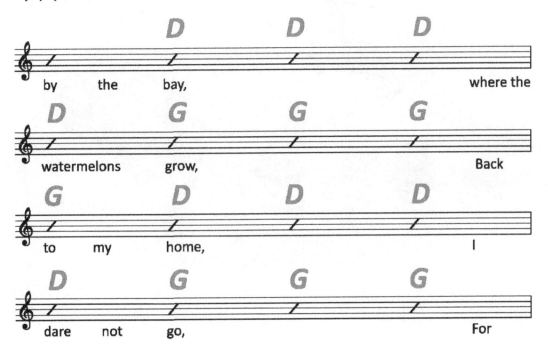

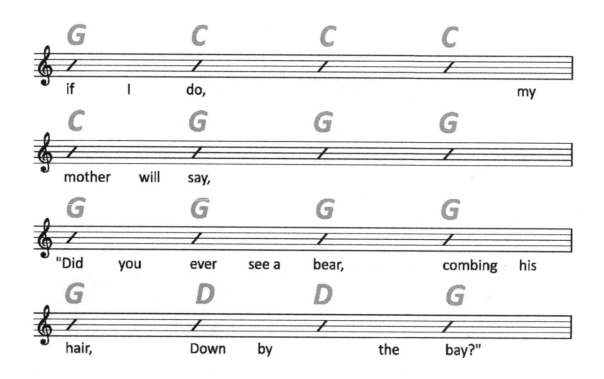

G   C   C   C

if   I   do,   my

C   G   G   G

mother   will   say,

G   G   G   G

"Did   you   ever   see a   bear,   combing   his

G   D   D   G

hair,   Down   by   the   bay?"

The following verses can be played using he same chords and rhythm.

Down by the bay, Where the watermelons grow,

Back to my home, I dare not go,

For if I do, My mother will say,

"Did you ever see a bee, With a sunburned knee,

Down by the bay?"

Down by the bay, Where the watermelons grow,

Back to my home, I dare not go,

For if I do, My mother will say,

"Did you ever see a moose, Kissing a goose,

Down by the bay?"

Down by the bay, Where the watermelons grow,

Back to my home, I dare not go,

For if I do, My mother will say,

"Did you ever see a whale, With a polka dot tail,

Down by the bay?"

Full Chords

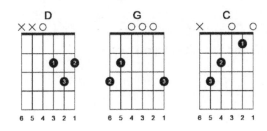

Audio/video available at www.justplay-music.com

SONG

Oh! Suzanna

G | G | G | G | G | G | D | D

I came from Ala - bama   with   my   banjo   on   my   knee,

G | G | G | G | G | D | G | G

I'm goin' to Lou - is - iana   my true   love   for   to   see;

G | G | G | G | G | G | D | D

It rained all night the day   I   left,   the weather it   was   dry;

G | G | G | G | G | D | G | G

The sun so hot I froze to death; Susanna,   don't you cry.

C	C	C	C	G	G	D	D

O, Susan - na, O, don't you cry for me,

G	G	G	G	G	D	G	G

I've come from Ala - bama with my banjo on my knee.

C	C	C	C	G	G	D	D

O, Susan - na, O, don't you cry for me, 'Cause I'm

G	G	G	G	G	D	G	G

goin' to Loui - si - ana, my true love for to see.

Full Chords

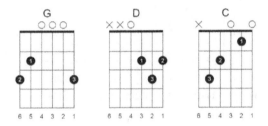

Section 6: Additional Lessons

Picking Song: Hot Crossed Buns

Like the previous picking lesson, you can use the same fingers as the fret numbers. So, when you see the 1st fret, use your 1st finger. When you see 3rd fret, use your 3rd finger.

Hot Cross Buns

Traditional

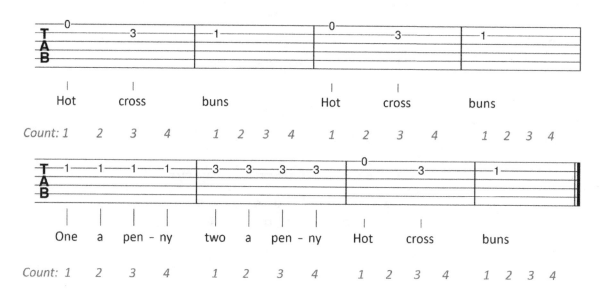

GREAT JOB!!

Picking Song: Twinkle, Twinkle Little Star

This next one is a little different as you will move up to the 5th fret in one part of this song. Slide your 3rd finger up from the 3rd fret to the 5th fret and back again when you get to that part. Try it in sections until you memorize it, then play the entire piece. See the picture below.

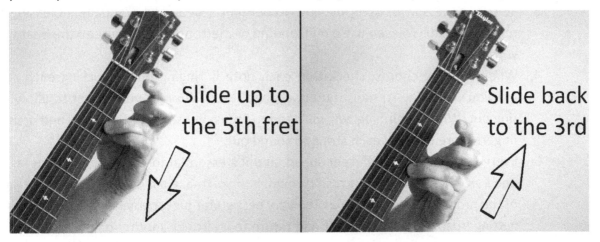

Twinkle, Twinkle, Little Star

Traditional

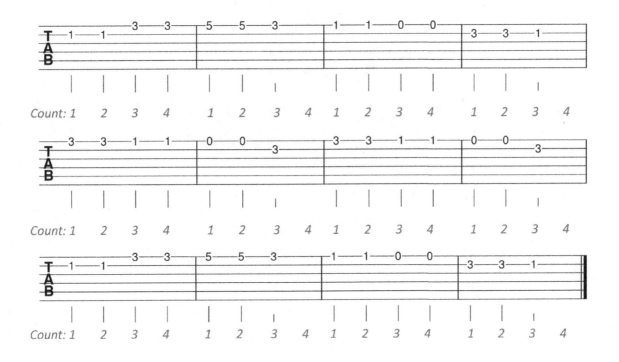

Audio/video available at www.justplay-music.com

Practise Tips

1. Start every practise by checking the tuning of your guitar.
2. Try to take a little time every day to practice. Even 10 minutes a day will show significant improvements over a week.
3. Start each lesson or song by slowly counting a beat and gradually increasing the tempo (speed). You can use a metronome or metronome app to keep the beat while you play.
4. When learning chords, check that each note is ringing out by picking each string individually. If any string is muted, change the position of your finger to allow it to ring out. When beginning, we will need to focus on using our fingertips and arch our fingers more to allow each string to sound out.
5. Everyone learns at a different speed, and it's essential to take as much time as you need on each lesson. Don't rush through it. If you make a mistake, it's ok! That is part of the process of learning. Even the very best guitar players make mistakes. If you are getting frustrated, take a break and return to it later or another day.
6. Also, if your fingers start hurting, take a rest. It will take some time until your fingers get used to the strings.

Have fun with it!! ☺

Audio/video available at www.justplay-music.com

Additional Exercises

A great way to warm up and improve finger agility, coordination and skill are to play some single note exercises. This can be scales or single-note songs and catchy melody lines.

Picking Exercises

This is a single note, open-string exercise to help us become more accustomed to playing the lower strings.

Picking Exercise 3
Play it through and repeat.

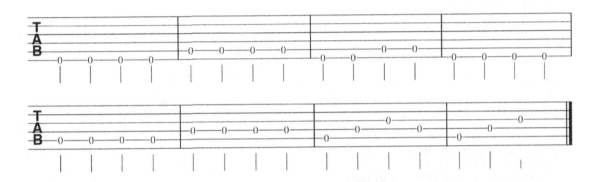

Scales

Scales are a great way to warm up before your lesson so I've included a couple to have in your practice routine. They can be played straight through and repeated as necessary. You can use the same fingers as the fret numbers indicated for both the following scales.

Picking Exercise 4: The C Scale

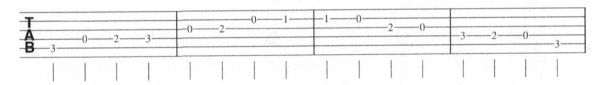

Picking Exercise 5: The G Scale

Audio/video available at www.justplay-music.com

Strumming Exercise 3: Mixed Patterns

A mixed strumming pattern includes using both downstrokes and upstrokes played rhythmically.

What is an upstroke? Instead of strumming downwards, strum upwards! It feels a lot different after practicing downstrokes. The blue arrow is the downstroke in the diagram, and the green is the upstroke.

Exercise 3.0
Strum on the count of one.
The "C" shows when to change the chord.

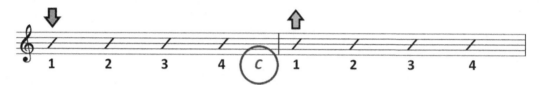

Exercise 3.1
Strum on the count of one and two.

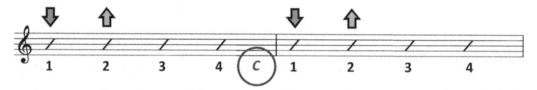

Exercise 3.2
Strum on the count of one and three.

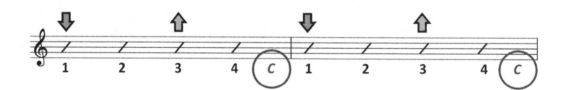

Exercise 3.3
Strum on every beat.

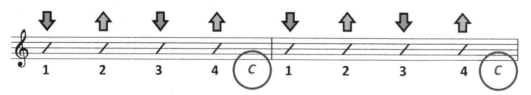

Strumming Exercise 4: Half-Beats & Mixed Patterns

These more-advanced strumming patterns focus on half-beats. Start them slowly and work your way up. Once you get the hang of it, they can be integrated into the songs you've already learned.

Exercise 4.0
Strum "down" on every beat and on every half beat. *(The beat inbetween)*

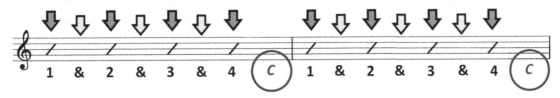

Exercise 4.1
Strum "down" on every beat and strum "up" on every half beat. *(The beat inbetween)*

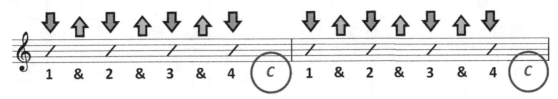

Exercise 4.2
Strum down on each arrow 1, &, 2, then strum up, then down again. And repeat.

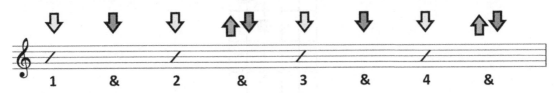

Common Chords Diagrams

Easy Chord Variations

G

G7
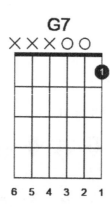

C
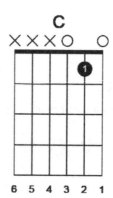

C variation

Full Chords

E
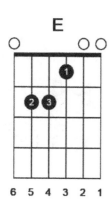

Em

D
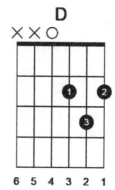

Dm
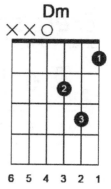

D7
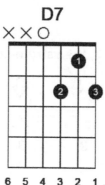

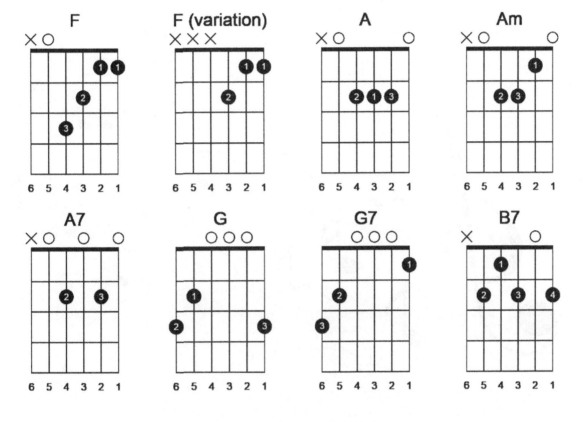

Common Fingering Variations

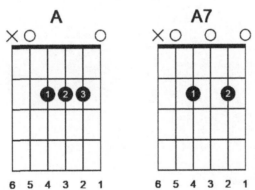

Student Practice Chart

You can use this sheet to keep track of practise time throughout the week and month.

Picking Exercise #1														
Picking Exercise #2														
Strumming Exercise 1.0 - 1.3														
Strumming Exercise 2.0 - 2.3														
Are You Sleeping (Brother John)														
Row, Row, Row Your Boat														
Mary Had a Little Lamb														
London Bridge is Falling Down														
Rain, Rain, Go Away														
A Tisket, A Tasket														
Hush Little Baby														
This Old Man														
The Wheels On the Bus														
Itsy Bitsy Spider														
He's Got the Whole World In His Hands														
Hokey Pokey														
She'll Be Coming 'Round the Mountain														
When the Saints Go Marching In														
Happy Birthday To You														
If You're Happy and You Know It														
Old MacDonald Had a Farm														
Twinkle, Twinkle, Little Star														
You are My Sunshine														
Down By the Bay														
Oh, Suzanna														
Picking Song: Hot Crossed Buns														
Picking Song: Twinkle, Twinkle, Little Star														
Strumming Exercise 3.0 - 3.3														
Strumming Exercise 4.0 - 4.2														

BLACKWOOD GUITARWORKS

CERTIFICATE OF COMPLETION

This Certificate is presented to

_____

For completing "*Just Play: Easy Beginner Guitar Lessons for Kids*".

_____
Parent/Teacher

_____
Date

93

Thank You, and One Last Thing

If you found this book useful, would you be kind enough to leave a short review? I depend on reviews to get the word out about my books! I also read all the reviews personally so that I can get feedback about how to make this, or future books even better. I'd love to hear how it's helped you.

Please leave a review at the retailer

you purchased this from.

Audio/video available at www.justplay-music.com

BLACKWOOD GUITARWORKS

Discover other books available from the author (paperback and digital editions):

Made in the USA
Las Vegas, NV
19 December 2024

14870922R00057